Naranjito

Pumpkin

Sea heart

Turpentine broom

Papaya

Guyanese wild coffee

Cocklebur

Strawberry

Japanese maple

Dandelion

Violet

Rice

Texas barberry

Coco de mer palm

Black palm

Mary's bean

Swamp palm

Date palm (extinct)

Hog plum

Hopseed

Hamburger bean

Slash pine

Teak

Red huckleberry

Sea coconut

Earpod

Orchid

Coast redwood

Indian almond

Corn

Bean

Monkey's comb

Sunflower

Texas mountain laurel

Milkweed

Devil's claw

Blueberry

Hopseed

To Rosemary Stimola, my "little flower," with gratitude and love —D. A.
To Sophie Grace, the sweetest little sprout in Nana's garden —S. L.

ACKNOWLEDGMENTS:

Victoria Rock, editor, and Sara Gillingham, book designer, for their incomparable vision and dedication to quality in children's books.

Steven Paton, Smithsonian Tropical Research Institute, Republic of Panama; Dr. Robert T. Harms, University of Texas at Austin;
Dr. Gerhard Leubner, University of Freiburg, Germany; Dr. Sarah Sallon, Natural Medicine Research Center, Jerusalem, Israel;
Carissa Nelson, Seed Technology Education Program, Colorado State University; Deborah Lewis, Ada Hayden Herbarium,
Iowa State University, Ames, Iowa; Steven Hurst, USDA–NRCA Plants Database; Matthew Sleigh, B and T World Seeds, Paguignan, France;
Megan Waters; Dr. Thomas L. Carlisle; Susette Newberry, PhD, Carl A. Kroch Library, Cornell University, Ithaca, New York; Robert Dirig,
L. H. Bailey Hortorium Herbarium, Cornell University (coco de mer image permission); Guy Eisner (date palm seed image);
Deborah Weist, National Park Service (redwood cones and seed images); Jo Cook, Urban Horticulture, University of Arizona;
Allan McDonald, British Columbia; Malcolm Storey, United Kingdom

Book design by Sara Gillingham and Katie Jennings.
Calligraphy by Anne Robin.
The illustrations in this book were rendered in ink and watercolor.
Manufactured in China.

Library of Congress Cataloging-in-Publication Data
Aston, Dianna Hutts.
A seed is sleepy / by Dianna Hutts Aston ; illustrated by Sylvia Long.
p. cm.
ISBN-13: 978-0-8118-5520-4
ISBN-10: 0-8118-5520-1
1. Seeds—Juvenile literature. I. Long, Sylvia, ill. II. Title.
QK661.A88 2007
581.4'67—dc22
2006013302

Distributed in Canada by Raincoast Books
9050 Shaughnessy Street, Vancouver, British Columbia V6P 6E5

10 9 8 7 6 5 4 3 2

Chronicle Books LLC
680 Second Street, San Francisco, California 94107

www.chroniclekids.com

A Seed Is Sleepy

by Dianna Hutts Aston · illustrated by Sylvia Long

chronicle books · san francisco

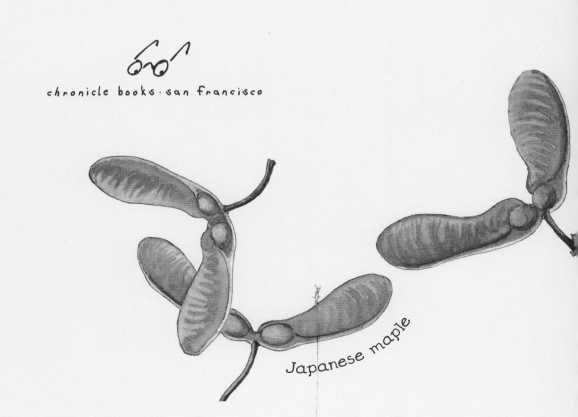

Japanese maple

Sunflower

A seed is sleepy.

It lies there, tucked inside its flower,
on its cone, or beneath the soil. Snug. Still.

Texas mountain laurel pod

A seed is secretive.

Texas mountain laurel seed

*It does not reveal itself
too quickly.*

Texas mountain laurel flower

Most seeds sleep through a season or two,
waiting for the warmer temperatures of spring.
But some take their time. Ten years might
pass before the bright red-orange seed of the
Texas mountain laurel shows its purple blooms.

Naranjito

Blueberry

A seed

Texas barberry

Papaya

Guyanese wild coffee

Indian almond

Turpentine broom

is fruitful.

strawberry

Devil's claw

Ninety percent of the plants on Earth are flowering plants. Flowering plants produce fruits—fruits of all shapes and textures that keep the seeds cozy until they have found the right place to grow.

A seed

Who would guess that a seed as small
as a freckle would grow into
the world's tallest tree? Only ten percent of
redwood trees begin as seeds, though.
Most redwood trees spring from existing trees.

is naked.

Yes, naked!

Scientists call gymnosperms—
seeds that aren't clothed
in fruits—naked seeds. Most
naked seeds hide themselves
on the scales of cones until
they're ready to make a dash
for the ground.

Coast redwood

350'

300'

250'

200'

150'

100'

50'

Seeds come

Orchid

The orchid seed is the smallest of all.
There might be a million seeds in one pod!
The seed of the coco de mer palm is the
largest. It can weigh up to 60 pounds.

in many sizes.

Coco de mer

Milkweed

Hopseed

A seed

Japanese maple leaf

Japanese maple seed

Hopseed

is adventurous.

It must strike out
on its own,
in search of a
less crowded place
to put down roots.

Milkweed

Dandelion

A parachute of fine, silky hairs
can take a dandelion seed 100
miles from its parent plant.

Mary's bean

Drift seeds float on
ocean currents, from one
shore to another.

Earpod

Sea heart

Monkey ladder pod

Swamp palm

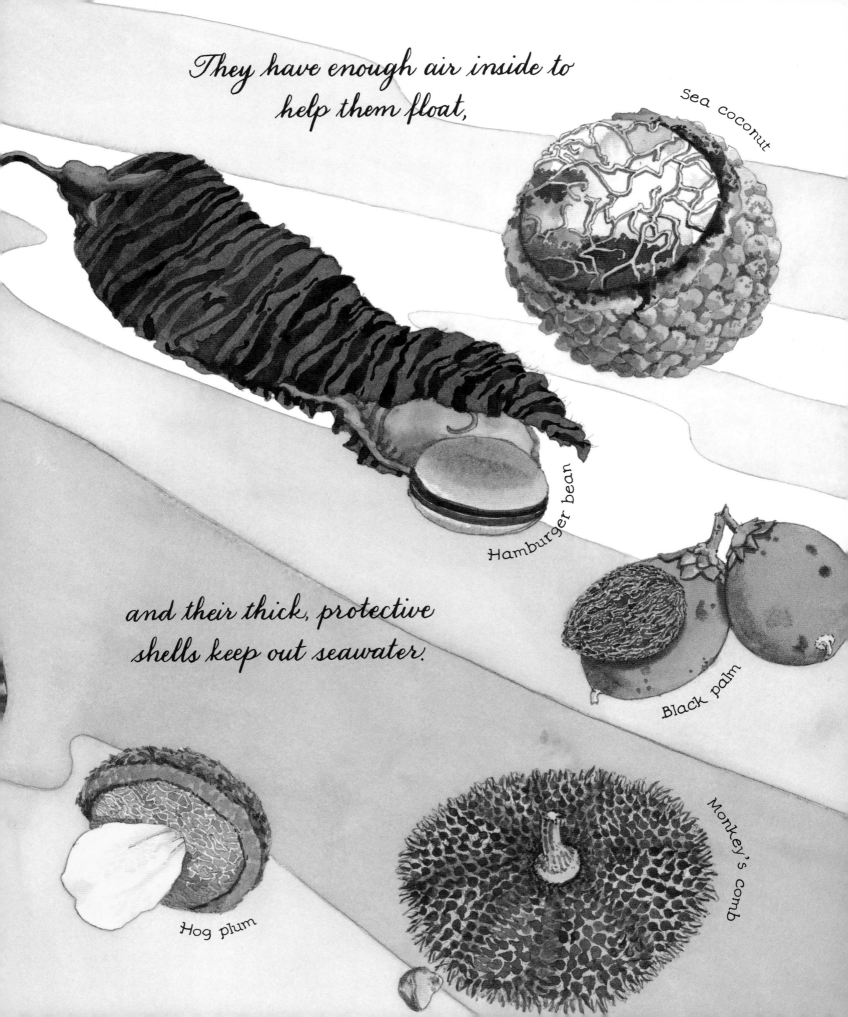

They have enough air inside to
help them float,

and their thick, protective
shells keep out seawater.

Sea coconut

Hamburger bean

Black palm

Monkey's comb

Hog plum

To find a spot to grow,
a seed might leap from its pod,

A seed

Violet

or cling to a
child's shoestring,

Cocklebur

is inventive.

*or tumble through
a bear's belly.*

Red huckleberry

A seed hopes to land where
there is plenty of
sunlight, soil, and water.

A seed is generous.

It gives the baby plant, or embryo,
a seed coat to keep it warm.

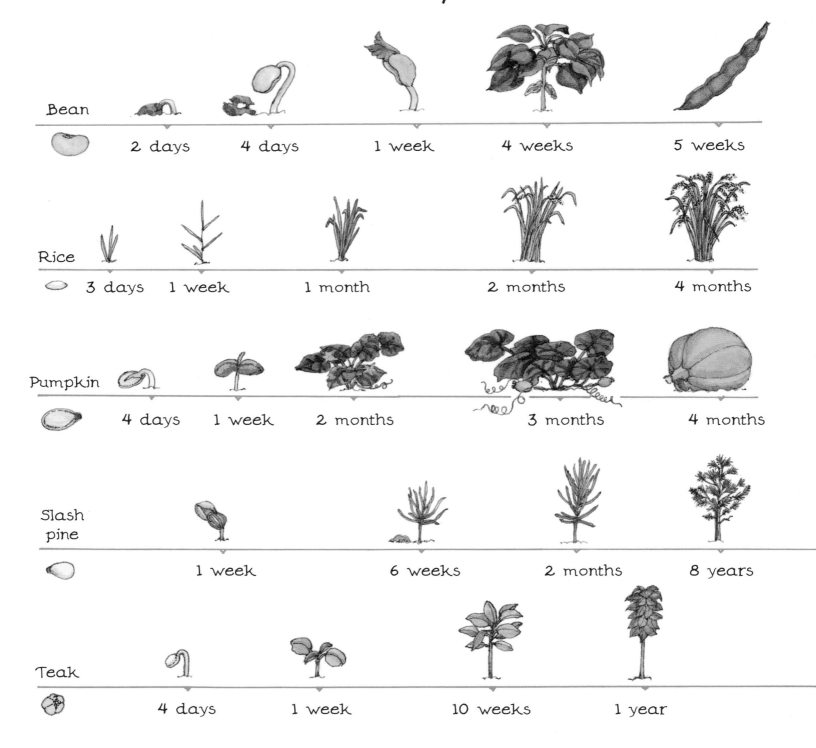

| Bean | 2 days | 4 days | 1 week | 4 weeks | 5 weeks |

| Rice | 3 days | 1 week | 1 month | 2 months | 4 months |

| Pumpkin | 4 days | 1 week | 2 months | 3 months | 4 months |

| Slash pine | 1 week | 6 weeks | 2 months | 8 years |

| Teak | 4 days | 1 week | 10 weeks | 1 year |

The embryo's first meal comes from its seed leaves, or cotyledons. Seeds with one seed leaf, like corn, are called monocots. Seeds with two seed leaves, like beans, are called dicots.

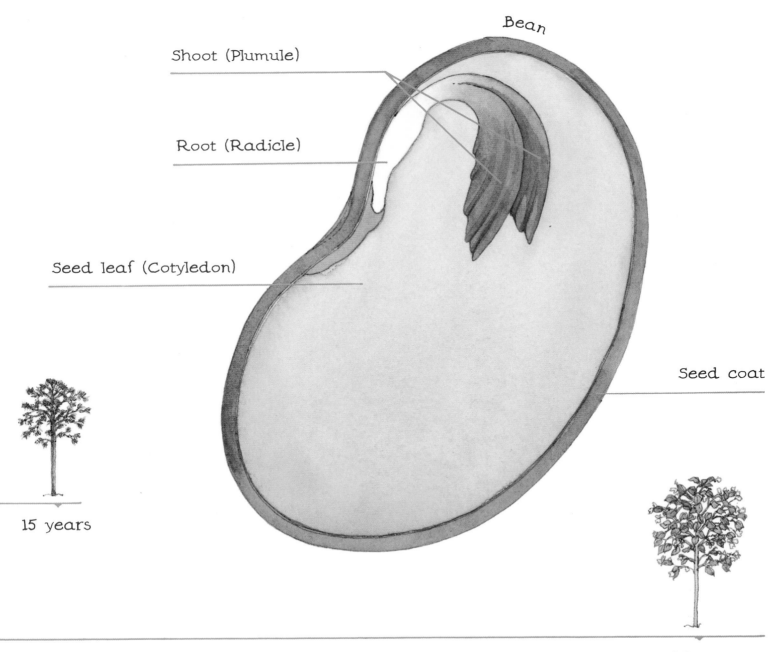

Bean

Shoot (Plumule)

Root (Radicle)

Seed leaf (Cotyledon)

Seed coat

15 years

100 years

Some seeds

Date palm

are ancient.

Not all seeds are eager to germinate.
Some have lain dormant, or slept undisturbed,
for more than a thousand years.

The oldest known seed to sprout
came from an extinct date palm tree.
After it was unearthed from a
long-ago king's mountaintop palace
in Israel, a scientist planted it.
Four weeks later, it sprouted!

A seed is thirsty

Bean

Part of the seed, the root, feels the tug of gravity and digs down deep.

. . . and hungry.

Once a seed has
shed its coat,
it drinks in the rain,
the dew, and
yesterday's icicles.
It feasts on
minerals in the soil.

Corn

Another part of the seed,
the shoot, is sensitive to light,
so it reaches for the sun.

A seed

Bean

Plants make their own food through a process called photosynthesis. Inside plant leaves are cells containing chemicals that absorb sunlight. Light gives them the energy they need to turn water and carbon dioxide—a gas in the air—into food.

is clever.

It knows to seek the sunlight...
to push itself up, up, up
through the soil. But it must
wait awhile before that happens.

Sunflower

A seed is sleepy,

but only until it has found
a place in the sun
and it has had its breakfast
and a drink of water.

Then a seed is . . .

awake!

Sunflower

Coco de mer palm

Turpentine broom

Cocklebur

Guyanese wild coffee

Violet

Slash pine

Corn

Indian almond

Sunflower

Earpod

Sea heart

Monkey ladder pod

Milkweed

Hog plum

Hopseed

Hamburger bean

Date palm (extinct)

Strawberry

Teak

Sea coconut

Mary's bean

Red huckleberry

Black palm

Texas barberry

Naranjito

Papaya

Orchid

Swamp palm

Texas mountain laurel

Bean

Monkey's comb

Dandelion

Blueberry

Coast redwood

Devil's claw

Pumpkin

Japanese maple

Rice